The Bones
of
Winter Birds

The Bones
of
Winter Birds

Ann Fisher-Wirth

Terrapin Books

© 2019 by Ann Fisher-Wirth
Printed in the United States of America
All rights reserved.
No part of this book may be reproduced in any manner, except for brief quotations embodied in critical articles or reviews.

Terrapin Books
4 Midvale Avenue
West Caldwell, NJ 07006

www.terrapinbooks.com

ISBN: 978-1-947896-11-6
LCCN: 2018963207

First Edition

Cover art: *La Pie*, by Claude Monet
Oil on Canvas, 1868–1869
Courtesy of Musée d'Orsay, Paris

for Peter

Contents

1
October: A Gigan	7
Mayumi	8
Vicksburg National Military Park	9
Prayer	10
Yoga Nidra	11
Cold Fire	12
Solstice	13
Team Teaching at Parchman, Mississippi State Penitentiary	14
In That Kitchen (She Speaks to Herself)	16
Again, California	17
Rain	18

2
Lace	21
Two Lives	23
The Frescoes of San Dalmazzo	24
Tenderness	26
Reading	28
Yugen	29
Sundown	30
Nearly April	31
Haecceitas	32

3   For Joan (1933-2017)
Why Not Left in Peace?	35
Her Days	37
The Right Loop Road	38
January 28	39
A Lacuna	41
Sister	42
Yahrzeit	44

4

Letter to Emma Bovary	49
Patio with Black Door	52
Minyas' Daughters	54
Shelterhouse	56
Everything Here Looks Very Dismal	57
We Came Home over the Snowy Fields for Christmas	58
The Witness	60
Beneath the Rain, the Pewter Feathers of the Seine	61
Liège, the Barges	62
Everything I Sculpted	63

5

Mississippi Invocation	67
Chant d'amour, 1965	68
Love Minus Zero	70
These Things	72
Golden Shovel with One Tomato	74
I Dreamed a Simple Story	75
Sumac	76
Wyrd	77
Sunlight, Sunlight	78
Return	79
Ascending *les Gorges du Chassezac*	81

Acknowledgments	83
About the Author	87

What falls away is always. And is near.

—Theodore Roethke, "The Waking"

1

October: A Gigan

Bamboo outside my window waves against the sky
where small birds warble, then grow silent, and the harsh

crows slice across the morning, across the pecan trees
exhausted from our Mississippi summer
when the air seemed nearly poison

and we could find no joy. The day is sweeter now
but sorrow gathers at every corner, across the world,

so much that the heart shuts down.
The Seer for the Evening at last month's party,

zipped up in a too-tight velvet costume,
waved a crimson fan before my face

and touching my temples said, *No joy shines in you.*
Cutting the cards, I drew
Balance   Gratitude   Breakthrough.

Breathe, and remember the fine-tipped leaves,
the quiet October air. Then it will come, the new.

Mayumi

Mayumi and I fell into the rhythms of working quietly together, she my sous-chef for that first Saturday dinner at the artist residency in California. We grated carrots by hand—a laborious process—making the carrot cake, not talking much as fog crept up the hills from the Pacific Ocean, and then I worked on shrimp and grits, wanting to bring them a bit of my Mississippi.

As we worked we spoke of the photographs Mayumi had just shown me in her studio, random families' snapshots largely destroyed by water after the Fukushima tsunami. Somehow she had found, scanned, and printed them so that they now are huge, about three feet by four, most of the colors gone. What colors remain are even more vivid, oranges and lime greens, ochers, with faces sometimes barely discernible. A shadowy child gazes out through time, in fractals of color and obliteration. Mayumi is making art of these photographs, cutting tiny petal-shaped holes or pinpricking from the reverse side so that you get a stippled texture, or cutting ever-decreasing V-shapes and gluing them one on top of another in infinitesimal mountains. What patience, doing that work—creating something haunted, beautiful, out of horrific damage.

She tested the cake for doneness as I stirred cheddar and salt into the bubbling grits. Outside wide windows, the redwoods darkened with evening. And beyond them, the hills, the silence— faraway through fog, the ocean.

Vicksburg National Military Park

When they were my sons,
I pulled the covers snug
around their ears
and tucked them in,
smoothed their hair,
kissed their salty eyelids.
Now gingko leaves
make golden blankets
around the tombstone
of a boy from Iowa
and another I can't read,
and another another
another another another
as far as I can see
scattered across the hillside
this autumn and every
autumn beyond counting.

Prayer

Let the mothers rush toward their babies
and wrap their arms around them tight enough
to hold back even the sea if it would harm them.

Let the anguish melt from the fathers' eyes.
This summer, the birds are going crazy with melody
in the jungle of wisteria and privet

that shelters my house, and at dawn the air
is fresh—there is sweetness in my life.
One Christmas Eve when our five were small

they asked to sleep on pallets so they could
be near the tree, these children of divorce
who came and went, who were apart from me

for months at a time. I sneaked into the room
just to be near the beloved tumble of arms
and legs, just to hear them breathe. That

bodily adoration. One whispered in her sleep,
one held her brother's toe, and the tree
with its shadowy packages loomed over them

in the dark, lit by a slant of light through the door.
When I first learned about war, I would
lie in bed brute with horror that a man

could tear a baby from its mother's arms.
That a man could *choose* to tear a baby
from its mother's arms. But so we see it now, each day.

Yoga Nidra

At the end they don't want to wake
though I murmur, *Move your fingers and toes,*

move your hands and feet, now let it travel
up your arms and legs, into the core of your body.

They lie in the sun on the astroturf
in the Grove, light and shade from the oaks

dappling their bodies, and I realize this is likely
the first real sleep they have had in months,

not a muscle moving, so quiet that I watch
one girl's belly to make sure she isn't dead,

so for some moments more I let them sleep.
Again I murmur, *Move your fingers and toes,*

until they respond. When we are all sitting
and have finished, they tell me that first time I spoke,

they never heard a thing. They carry such weight,
my students. One girl comes to class having just

encountered her ex who beat her up last year,
another grieves for her fiancé shot in August,

a guy tells me his mother's cancer is back
and they have no insurance, some work

all-night shifts at WalMart and still can't pay the rent.
Rising oceans, melting icecaps, neonics, the endless wars—

After yoga nidra, they trail off through the trees.

Cold Fire

> Charlotte Bronte's *Villette*, Lucy Snowe

Now you come again into grief's winter.

Here your history waits for you. Here the woman
with black tulips sits you down at the worn

deal table, bids you watch through the empty window.

Look at the stubble fields, where the starved owl hovers
over mud and scanty snow. Look at the sun,

swallowing the jackdaws as they rise...

Why not get a cat? After all, why be lonely?
Why not have a child, eat roasted apples by the fire—

instead, a life spent teaching pupils, reading letters

you save from Paul, from far across the ocean,
three years' letters, like touches on your cheek,

to see you through. Snow beneath snow, Lucy.

Once he called you *spitfire, she wild creature;*
once he made you blush.

Now, sure as salt, this day has come again for you.

Solstice

This morning I lay beside my husband,
eyes turned to the window,
and watched a cardinal, a splash of vermilion
in the rimed privet. I thought, this, at least,
is beautiful, this bright eye
and the brain I cannot begin to imagine,
in these days of fear, this blood-bright bird
among the icy leaves,
as the creatures, as the children perish.

Now we go into the woods.
Now we go into the shadows.
The path through these hills
is muddy with suffering.

Team Teaching at Parchman, Mississippi State Penitentiary

Scatters of little gray birds flutter back and forth
across the high barbed fence,
and after a rainy month the bare Delta prison yard
is splotched with green.

I crane my neck to see if the men
in their green and white striped pants
are crossing the macadam from the ward.
Not yet. Not yet to come to this large gray room

and read each other stories of their lives.
I do not know these men beyond our hours.
I know they do not have AC,
even in the Mississippi summer,

and the one fan, an old-style box, does little,
so when they write on the ward,
their sweat pools on the page.
I know they have grandmas,

because they tell about grandmas.
One of them writes about
killing a high-placed Klansman.
Some write copiously. Others, in fragments.

Smooth moves with the ladies,
ominous dreams, near-death accidents,
longings for their children. Lockdowns.
Strip searches, being shunted in trucks

in cages from place to place.
But no matter what they've done,
no matter how beaten down
they sometimes look when they arrive,

as the hours pass, laughter comes.
Halting or in a rush, words come.
They listen to each other, bear each other up.
As a guy in Big Mike's story says, *You feel me?*

In That Kitchen (She Speaks to Herself)

> *Oh Christ, that night should come so soon.*
> —William Carlos Williams

You grew up in a kitchen where salt and pepper arrived in corncob shakers and oil and vinegar dressing lived in a cruet with a little skirt. Gingham curtains, starched and bleached and pressed free from all grease and smoke, fluttered in good morning America. But that was a kitchen that never interested you, a kitchen of mom and Chuck and little Davie, of Rex the cocker spaniel, and Bluet the parakeet. It's gone now, gone, gone, gone. Smoke stains the blue corridors. Chuck joined the Army and was killed in Vietnam. Little Davie bought a motorcycle. Thank God, he learned to think for himself—now he's a doctor in Tangiers.

Think of the lies you were told about sex and history and America. Think of the body. It wants to lie all open, salt-stained, rain-scarred, the body wants its forgetfulness and honey. You rock back and forth, shoulders hunched, smoke rising from the one cigarette you allow yourself, stained, scarred woman, good morning America now gone, guns massed at the borders once again, churches burning, dogs howling, you in the private theatre of your own film *noir*.

In that kitchen, despite the official sunshine, soup boiled up with the bones of winter birds, cook-sweat slid down the windows, and the mothers cooked the death of things. That is a role you do not need, not in this world of ruined cities. Put your jacket on, walk out, take to the beds of lovers. The Never Rains Always Pours corncob shakers are clogged with bones and feathers and ash. The forests are falling. Toxic sludge slows down the rivers, toxic smoke drifts through the air. Take to the streets of this our America.

Again, California

First the crows over the scorched grasses
the vivid sun and cicadas singing

then fog seeps up from the coast
beyond the hills where now deer browse

quiet as stones in the gathering night.

Rain

I have returned to this loft among redwoods
in the California mountains.
Gradually the night steadies itself around me.
Outside, the tiniest rain begins to heal the desiccate hills.

Rain, small sweet rain, bringing these hills of my childhood
back to tenderest green. I have carried so much fear
that those I love will suffer. As they will.

Pools begin to gather where quail nest in the darkness.
I think we are provided for,
said my dying friend when I asked him
if he sensed what lies beyond pain.

2

Lace

    1946. For my parents

1.

He screams once.
Just once.

She holds him, strokes his back
as his heart thuds through sweat-soaked pajamas

against her bridal nightgown,
the fawn-colored silk she bought in the city

after work one winter day,
folded in tissue in a drawer,

and saved three years, until she knew
he would be coming home to her.

Sometimes she opened the drawer,
unwrapped the tissue, stroked the bodice,

and ran the satin straps between her fingers,
then read once more the letters

Army censors had cut to lace
lest they reveal the slightest information.

Dearest, It is _____
and we have now _____ for

_____ *where soon we will* _____.
All she knew was that he loved her.

2.

And as she strokes him,
his nightmares of bodies in ditches, and stench,

and flies crawling over eyeballs,
everything he passed on the road when the Army

retook Manila, slowly recede from him
into the netherworld where he will, by force,

beat them back and conceal them
the whole length of their marriage.

The train carries them deep
and deeper into the mountains where, from their roomette,

he turns his head toward the window
to watch snow fall, clean and silent, through the darkness.

Two Lives

Over and over in that green bedroom shadowed by the olive tree, I went to her bureau, slid open the top drawer with its carved roses to sneak eye shadow, mascara. I opened the underwear drawer, lifted and let fall the soft white things, the taupe stockings folded in whispery tissue. I stroked the shawl in the bottom drawer, being careful not to roughen with my fingers the embroidered ivory silk with knotted fringe. Of this shawl she told me once, *This was my mother's, from my father. But before my mother could wear it, her mother-in-law blew her nose on it.* I sat on the bed, helped her zip the gold dress she made for date nights with my father at the San Francisco opera, opened the little vial with metallic powder, dusted the faintest sparkle of gold in her hair.

Over and over in that green bedroom shadowed by his collapse and illness, I rummaged the drawers of his highboy, shuffled black socks and blue Balbriggan pajamas. White handkerchiefs, bright medals, cigarette box engraved with his Army ID. The letters were not there yet—love letters from him, from Wetzlar and Fulda; she must have put them there many years after he died. *We have barely bread for some. All day I interview prisoners. I pretend you are here; we sit on a balcony and watch the sun set over these German hills. Then I cook for you, a nice salmon filet. I miss you as much as I love you, and that is saying a lot.* I love this shyness, the emphasis on food—

Once when he lay dying he peed the bed. He struggled to a chair. She changed the sheets, put him in fresh pajamas. I heard them from the hall, then she was hurrying to the store and as she passed before the bureau, he whispered, *You should find another man.* She wheeled on him for the first time ever. *Damn it, John, do you think there's anyone else?*

When I found these letters the year of her death, I could barely unfold them. They burned in my hands like foxfire.

The Frescoes of San Dalmazzo

You see here treasure, said the ex-Mayor
of Cigliè—*frescoes of the Passion,
painted in 1573 by the Master of Cigliè.*
We gathered to listen—the husbands, my daughter
holding the baby, I with an eye on little Benji.

*See here the donor, dressed as a Crusader,
kneeling with San Dalmazzo. On the ceiling,
the beautiful Annunciation, modeled after
Michelangelo.* God zapping Mary
with a beam of light as an angel watches.

And here—he turned to the left—*as I have
never seen elsewhere, the gouged eyes
of Christ's tormentors; look where the villagers
used chisels, nails, knives, the eyes
exist no more or even the faces entirely.*

Three soldiers casting lots for the clothes,
another leering, lifting a sponge
of vinegar and hyssop as he teetered
on a ladder next to Christ bending down
from the Cross—paint and plaster hacked

and slashed, *Ecce! Ecce! Ecce!*
so that never again would they witness
the twinned tenderness of hazelnuts,
velvety and scrotal outside the chapel
on the spreading summer trees, never again

glimpse a flash of scarlet beneath the hedges
and stoop to pluck and eat wild strawberries.
And look at Satan, the ex-Mayor said,
*he flies from the sky to rip the soul
from the bloody entrails of hanging Judas.*

He cannot take the soul from the mouth—
having kissed our Lord, even in betrayal
the mouth is blessed. Benji was bored,
he wanted to race on the stones and rub his hands
along the frescoes, so I took him outside

where he peed a proud two-year-old's pee
into some grasshopper grasses. And the people
of Cigliè went home four hundred years ago,
and were as people always are—
some cruel, some kind, drinking wine, sopping bread.

Tenderness

When I wake, afraid,
the light on the deck next door
where the frat boys live
who have tumbled into sleep
after much beer
and after sprinting up and down
the street with their
black Labs, chasing frisbees,
calling, *Yo, got it man*—
the light they forgot to flick off
after grilling burgers
on the deck, just like they forget
to water their yard or take
their garbage cans off the street—
this random, ordinary light
shines among the inky trees
and through the thick
music of locusts and tree frogs
as if to call me home,

like a candle in the window
of a fairy tale cottage
at the heart of the *dunkel,
dunkel Wald*—or the safety
I felt when I was small, when
my little sister and I would sleep,
legs curled around legs and heads
pillowed against the doors
in the back seat of the green
Chrysler, as our mother
rested her cheek on her hand
and hummed peacefully
out the side window,
and our father drove through

the cool September night from
the Tuscarora Mountains—
then I would wake groggy
to see the garage light
waiting for us, and one of them
would carry me up to bed.

Reading

> *And, you away, / As with your shadow I with these did play*
> —William Shakespeare

I was fifteen, in Berkeley. I sat on my bed in that third-story room, its white curtains patterned with pink roses. I was doing something solitary and adult, something the world would not expect of me—not, for once, schoolwork, but tackling sentences beyond what I had ever experienced. For fifteen minutes between homework and dinner, I read, baffled and summoned, about a woman who read to a boy, and a man who came and stood near them and said of the weather, *It won't be fine*, like cold water thrown on them where they sat.

I read this because my mother gave it to me, when I told her I was bored. The twilight sun coming in through my windows high above the bay lit up my room with such a glow as one scarcely lives through. I was not only enraptured, but also lost because I had no idea what was going on. Those sentences swooped and dived and did not light, like seabirds, the mind free to go the strangest places, the wedge-shaped core of darkness, and Mrs Ramsay felt invincible as long as she held a child and felt its head warm and live beneath her chin. Then, let them say what they liked, they could not harm her.

Mrs Ramsay was Woolf's mother, and how Woolf felt about her mother was how I felt about my mother, this adoration so far beneath personalities it might as well have been rocking on the moon. Rocking in the womb. And when Mrs Ramsay reads the sonnet, sitting with Mr Ramsay in the library after dinner, it's as if she is foretelling her own death, the death that will happen suddenly, soon, in parentheses. *From you have I been absent in the spring . . .* she reads. *From you have I been absent in the spring . . .* Virginia writes, speaking to a ghost, creating out of shadows the mother she lost when she was thirteen.

Yugen

> Mystery, darkness, beauty—the essence of Noh,
> in which ghosts often appear in a vision or dream

Now you creep back into this room you love,
silent, cold, with the night sea encircling,
to garnets that flow from your jewelry box
down the black table. Small fire—and your hands,
unappeased, remember the world,
remembering red. Before this loneliness.

Now let us make it as it used to be.
A room where we can sit, where we're at home.
Let us unfold these strange, upholstered chairs
for which you made the pillows long ago.
Pillows the color of wheat, and amber,
topaz, snowy, golden—smooth or slubbed silk—

Somehow they also fold up to nothing.
Let us arrange the chairs for conversation,
the ones lined against the walls like chairs
on an abandoned stage set, left behind
when you went wherever it was, shut down
the house, shut down your breath, shut down your eyes.

Sundown

She came through the door
while I stood at the stove carefully shaking cayenne

into the chicken noodle soup, and there she was
in her white nightgown. *Mama* I said,

it is you, your own face and body—
and she grinned at me as she never grinned in life.

Cicadas whirred in the privet. A bullfrog plunked
the opening notes of summer. The final bits of sunlight

like a jointed delicate spider
glimmered through the melancholy trees.

I said, *I will give you anything you want, I will
do anything for you because here you are.*

She replied, *Just let me be near you.* So I turned
from the stove and led her into the little green bedroom

where, propped on pillows, she could watch me
like a child as I moved about the kitchen.

As I pulled the quilt up, her warm, imperceptible hand
began to stroke my cheek. *It's all right, it's all right.*

Nearly April

Look at the wisteria, twining up the oaks
and beeches, flowing down in ghostly
rivers of purple blossom,
look at the redbud, its tiny crimson petals
opening out like blood drops right on the branch,
hectic and lacy in late afternoon light,
look at the last daffodils that will
be gone, legend says, by the night the tomb
opened—and think of the children newly dead—
it is the oldest thing in the world, to ask
how spring could consent to break once more
when mothers and fathers—but that's just it,
the sap-rife glory does not stop for grief.

Haecceitas

>   after Christopher Smart

For the tomato is an orb of holy light.

For its seeds are the defenders of heaven.

For if the vine grow freely it will scale the vault of the stars.

3

For Joan
(1933-2017)

Why Not Left in Peace?

To the Lighthouse

She sits all day in a double-wide in Bend, as dust

felts the sixty-six glass paperweights, blue and teal and turquoise,
some with gold stars,
                 some with aquatic swirls,
arranged in spirals in both shelves of her coffee table.

What are the diseases that have blossomed in her blood?
        She warns us when we phone her,
              You'd better not call my doctor.

Who was the father she never saw past infancy?
              And how did she feel, already
half grown, getting another dad?

I wrote her letters
        when she was in the Army.   *I saw a movie*
               about a horse. I read a Nancy Drew
        about a girl who found a clock.

But the code for our family was silence.

For decades our mother kept saying,
                She loves children.
      I wish she'd meet a nice man.

I think of Joan's life in Bend. The porch with months of recycling,
        craft room too stuffed to enter—

twenty-four glue sticks, five-foot row of marking pens,
wrapping paper, rubber stamps,
plastic tubs spilling scraps of paper, and hundreds

                of handmade greeting cards she never
sold or gave away.

Last year I planned to visit again.
> But she phoned the week before. *You better not come.*
> *It might snow.*

Yet, when I was eighteen, her tenderness—
she opened the bathroom door where I was hiding.
Mother told me, she said.

> She didn't say the word *pregnant,*
> > just picked up the book I'd dropped.

Don't worry, Annie, she said.
Someday you'll write a book like Virginia Woolf.

Her Days

I imagine her seventy-five years ago, with yellow hair ribbons, running across the meadow to where Great-Uncle Henry saddled his palominos and redwing blackbirds sang from the fence posts in Boone County.

Now she sits in her blue fuzzy slippers, a liter bottle of Pepsi cradled in the crook of her arm, and twenty-one crossword puzzle books piled up behind her. For three years now she hasn't weeded her garden, that weedy patch beside her trailer, because *I don't know, I just feel blah.*

Her cat Midnight likes to curl on the shelf by the signed John Grisham first editions. Joan's reading Harry Potter because she got it cheap. She lives on social security because she spent all her retirement fund in one glorious year traveling the country in a double-wide with Shirley.

Once, when I was a kid, I watched her bowl with her team, wearing her bowling shirt, white with *Mel's* stitched in orange on the pocket. Another time I watched her play pool, sinking her shots and looking up with a sly, shy smile. She let me share her Pepsi and chalk her cue.

She was so good she won a dishwasher.

Now she sleeps sitting because her ribs hurt, and drives everywhere, even a block away, because her legs hurt. Her skin is like crushed petals, so soft, so kindly, or like withered apples.

She taught me the ABC's. But when I was a child, she was mostly away at college.

Her red sweater transfixed me, I've been told, when newborn I came from the hospital. I have a picture of her holding me, her hair pulled sideways in a tortoiseshell barrette.

The Right Loop Road

We liked the gentle joke of three sisters,
rarely together, having lunch in the town
called Sisters. So we bundled her and her
wheelchair/walker contraption in the car

and drove north through gathering snow
toward the café we had been assured
had delicious soup and doughnuts. But
we could not find it and pushed her block

after block, colder and colder, finally
discovering a door through which a burly
passerby had to lift her, chair and all.
After the not-good soup and doughnuts,

we drove back to Bend and got lost.
Early dusk had fallen, with snow slanting
across the windshield, and her slumped
lower and lower in the front seat, moaning.

The body in pain is a terrifying thing.
Desperately we wanted to find the right
loop road, find the assisted living,
get help, get her into her warm dry bed.

January 28

And you a thousand miles away
in that narrow bed where they have
treated you kindly. Your lungs fill,
your breath rasps, your forehead
scorches the caretaker's hand as she
lays cool cloths upon it. When she
phoned and said perhaps you could
still hear me, I talked to you, but what
was there to say? I called back,
and called back, again and again.
Now the hours pass. I return
to the years when you taught me
to read, or when you ran in the highway
to save my little bear, or when you brought
your friend Carol home from college
and next day, approaching your bedroom,
I saw you suddenly sit up and knew
you loved girls, though it took you
thirty more years to say. I don't know
if you were lonely. Last time we visited—
your sisters, our husbands—we all sat
in your room and went again through
the cards on which you had fastened
the remnants of your button collection.
Since there was nothing to talk about,
we played the game of *which three buttons
do you like best?* There never was much
to talk about, was there? love, but few words.
Tonight I am lighting candles for you.
Once an hour, she said, they give you
morphine. Today the sun was everywhere,

and I trailed behind my grandchildren
wobbly on their bikes, I held their hands
to cross the streets. You never met them,
and now all things will remain unsaid.
But I am talking to you now, my sweet
sister, I don't want to stop talking to you,
my thoughts keep time with your breathing.

A Lacuna

What if I feel no grief
when the grief counselor phones
and leaves a message, expects I am
sobbing how sudden it was—

when the grief thudded to the ground
and shriveled long ago,
and her death was anything
but sudden, ever since they found her

in the icy bathtub, unconscious,
forty-eight hours since she had fallen or
whatever happened; and luckily
her friends peeked through the window

when she did not show up
for pool or bowling or whatever
hobby group. That was years
ago and before that, my sweet sister,

what was her life like—
I can see I'll have to phone back,
the grief counselor just phoned
again, do I need grief literature,

no, do I need counseling, no,
I can love my sister without ever
really knowing her, the time
for knowing my sister passed long ago.

Blessings to her. Blessings
in her transformation to ash,
to spirit, scattered handfuls of memory,
not much, it slips between my fingers.

Sister

Deadeye Duke they called her when she was a WAC in Alabama. Today, driving by a shooting range here in the Ozarks, I thought of her. *Not to brag or anything*, she told us way back in the 1960's, *but your big sister is the best shot in her platoon.* We were in awe of her. She had to make her bed so tight she could bounce a dime on the mattress. She had to wear white gloves and run her hands along the bureau. And once she had to swim *fast*, to escape a water moccasin that came gliding from the pipe in the Fort McClelland pool.

Then tonight, at the restaurant, an old woman entered pushing a walker, and a younger woman followed, hanging on to the back of her pants to steady her. They sat down close to us. I watched them and remembered our sister less than a year ago, like a shrunken little elf, grinning up at us from her plate piled high with Thanksgiving dinner in the restaurant in Bend where snow blew in flurries outside. The next morning was the last time I saw her, and I knew it would be. I turned back from the front door of the house where they cared for her, and went again to her room to give her one more kiss. She was just lowering herself from her walker into her chair.

We found her journal in that freezing cold garage after her death. I took it and glanced at the first page, shocked at the savage, cutting words, thinking, *Who could say that about you?* until I realized she had written it about herself.

I knew thirty years before she finally told our mother, and I knew why *it just never took* when she wore her teal blue dress and went on dates with *nice men from church*. Yet because she was so private, I never could tell her, *I love you just the way you are.* So when I read in her journal about that woman who did not love her back, how she hated herself, despised herself, for wanting that love, I was furious for her misery.

Gentle sister, sweet sister, I say this now to her memory—just, *Gentle sister, sweet sister—*

Yahrzeit

The sun shone bright today
as it shone the day you died,
when we kept phoning just
to hear you breathe, and they
said you heard us, too. It's
almost as if you never were,
you never wanted to be known,
politely pushing us away until
we had to go and help you.
In that double-wide with years
of papers stacked beneath
the porch—*oh, don't take
the recycling, it can stay there*—
you piled your kitchen floor
with boxes of food and your
refrigerator with styrofoam
containers of half-eaten food,
and the floor by your chair
with a knee-high stack of
crossword books which I will
be doing for years, and your
closet with jigsaw puzzles and
your drawers with 300 pairs
of socks. But what does this
tell anyone of you? Or that
your rugs were so full of grit
vacuuming them
was like vacuuming the beach?
I am burning a *yahrzeit* candle
for you, my stubborn, lonely
sister, on this first anniversary
of your death. For the rest
of my life, I will be wearing
your diamond ring and sometimes
the gold earrings you never wore,
and I will save the two sheets

of buttons I kept from your huge
collection, golden or jeweled
or cloisonné buttons attached
to white cardboard in a diamond
pattern of black-inked squares.
When we had little to talk about,
we would look through the drawer
where all the button sheets were piled
and play the game of *which is
your favorite button?* Mine,
my love, is the smallest, half
as big as my pinkie nail—a circle
of bronze, within it a circle of white,
at the center an aqua translucent orb—
like a nest with a robin's egg.

4

Letter to Emma Bovary

1

Emma, my students don't like you.
The women think they see through you, the men

just want to make you. No one mutters,
Emma, c'est moi. You're bad with money,

sick with romance,
you shove your little Berthe so she falls and cuts her head

just because she toddles up to hug you.
Even your suicide botched,

the arsenic eating your guts. Vomiting, screaming
with pain. You thought it would be beautiful.

2

As a girl I sat by the window, dreaming,
face in my hands, eyes unfocused
on the spiky leaves
in the thicket before me.

My holy vow, like yours, to languish
in the dream of how I loved
myself—swathed in poufs of silk,
staring into the flames of two tall candles.

Now I scurry through the days,
dust rag in one hand, checklist in the other—

                This February midnight,
I'm wondering where you've gone. When did I get
so *good*?

3

Your tongue flicks out to taste the final sweetness
in the liqueur glass.

When you balance on the wet stones, laughing,
the field is yours, all paths

are yours, your parasol teeters gaily
in the sunlight, your skirts caress your legs
as they flow and swirl around you.

You run across the dew-soaked grass
early in the morning.

You turn to him with little cries.
His voice is full of sleep.

                    But Rodolphe
buries that scrap of paper
in the basket of apricots, and gallops off,
abandoning you.

4

It all comes back to an empty field, winter twilight,
the greyhound escaped from your carriage

and vanished forever behind the line of trees—
and the terror that rises in your throat then.

It all comes back to woodlice crawling
out of frozen firewood, the plaster priest

crumbling all winter in your garden.
And soup, slurped soup.

Your desire and desolation. Your furious silence,
as well-meaning Charles smiles and swallows.

5

Here's what you do not know:

Your life melts around you
like moonbeams.

Your daughter
will starve in the cotton mill.

After you die, dumb faithful Charles
will gather a lock of your hair.

His scissors will snick
your neck, as bloodless as paper.

Patio with Black Door

Georgia O'Keeffe

1

Adobe wall and door,
four rhomboids of sunlight,
and in the upper left a wedge of sky—

in Abiquiu, in August,
even the lizards seek shelter
when mirage shakes the desert like fever—

nothing but water and earth.
Nothing holds desert at bay
like the smooth, shadowed flank
of this adobe.

2

Because you are far
from home, you imagine shelter
and tell yourself a story
about inside. Apricots ripen, tawny
against the worn adobe.
Carp glint like sullen flames
beneath the moss-green pads of lilies.
Gaunt in long black cotton, a crooked-fingered woman
stitches a fine seam
in the blue lace dress she sews
for the statue of the Virgin.
Her dog, half coyote, thumps his tail
and dreams of rabbits—the old quick chase
through the creosote. His lips twitch
as he sprawls in a spill of sunlight.

3

Out of the earth they come,
and all things gather their separate radiance.
In Abiquiu, in August,

flecks of quartz and mica—the least
barbed quill, the ice-fine needle aureoles
around the barrel cacti—leaf-green, poppy-red,
mustard-flower-golden
splotches, scales, and claws of every mountain boomer
blaze in this dizzying light.

4

But the door—

as if a woman
opened her dark dress
to show you heat
and tenderness
and sleep

while around her, viridian leaves
shifted and turned in the dappled summer.

The carp wait sleepless in the moonlight.
Heavy with nectar, the apricots wait.
Crickets among the branches
begin to chant, incessantly chafing and stirring,

and you stand
before the patio's
black door.

Minyas' Daughters

> from Ovid's *Metamorphoses*

I understand their *no* when all of Thebes
runs frenzied, crying after Dionysus. They love the loom—

> *I woke from a sound sleep at 3 a.m. whimpering*
> *"I don't want to." Don't want to what?*

hypnotic shuttle of threads rising and falling, greeny-
gold and burnished purple flowers unfolding on the loom.

> *Don't want to scrape it down to bone. I have done*
> *enough damage with desire for one lifetime,*

They love the sister-bond of stories, one girl's leading
to the next, gods embracing maidens, lust and loss and gloom.

> *and what is "the Dionysian" anyway: the stiletto-heeled*
> *staggering-drunk underage girls hanging on to each other,*

They love quiet and to work. But *this* god demands release.
Outside, the streets run red. Cries of orgy vex the room.

> *laughing and shrieking as they stagger from one bar*
> *to the next Thursday nights on the Square,*

The weavings turn to vines, blooms to bulging grapes; sweet
scents of myrrh and saffron, and crimson flames consume

> *or the sex on torn couches back at the frat house?*
> *Why would a god command that? Ghazals express*

all reason—spurned, the god makes wild beasts howl,
   panthers scream,
and turns girls to bats: juddering, squeaking, in twilight gloom—

> *a longing for ecstasy and God, and I long for ecstasy*
> *and God but only partly. I love quiet and to work.*

Still, till night comes Minyas' stubborn daughters will be weaving, their voices drifting softly back and forth across the room.

Shelterhouse

She walked beyond the village as children played
            with their teacher, to enter the mountain forest
        where fir trees loomed and ice covered the ground—

ice flowing in the dim dream light, strangely
            like flesh, not cold— where nearly translucent
        slabs of stone with runic carvings swayed
from the limbs of shadow-blackened trees.

            And she fell to her knees, beginning to stroke
        the swooping ice-covered flanks of the living
mountain that sheltered the living and the dead—
            beginning to stroke the sleek, shadowy,

        death-encompassing mountain with its looming trees
and nearly isinglass hanging gravestones. Suddenly
        she was weeping, paying homage to the mountain
        that opened forever beyond her knowing.

Palest stone, the wrist-thin enormous slabs
        swaying from the trees, inscribed with names
    of the dead in a language she could not see
to read. The shelterhouse, and she wanted

        to move further and further into it,
    up the mountain with its jade-smooth mounded
flesh-ice, and she worshiped and adored it.

Everything Here Looks Very Dismal

But if there were rabbits, clustered beneath the chestnut trees, uncanny in twilight. If there were ancient wooden houses, and kitchen gardens stretching toward the tracks, with knobby cabbages or trellises of beans that cast long shadows as the train clattered by. If women moved slowly back and forth, scattering feed from battered pails, if chickens flustered up clucking, pecking, with their curious hitch gait. If men came from the barns in muddy boots, bulky sweaters tucked into their overalls, and scraped their boots, entered their kitchens, shut their blue doors.

If night came down as we gazed out the window, if fields folded themselves like cloaks and sank into sleep. If we sank into sleep. And if we rode on the train as summer passed, then autumn, as it carried us into the mountains, till we came to a river so cold it burned. If we crossed it asleep on stepping stones, flapping our gawky wings.

We Came Home over the Snowy Fields for Christmas

a fantasy of la Bête du Gevaudan

Then the great halls were thrown open.
The lady of that place gave everyone a gift—
cakes stiff with age, hoarded in the larder.
Sachets that had lingered in a drawer,

now little but dust and brittle lavender.
Tracts no one could read, on the techniques
of draining marshes. Like me
a poor relation, Marie-Claude was there,

and after we stroked each other's cheeks,
we climbed the attic stairs
to sit by the dressmaker dummies,
one still wearing a blouse that Marie-Claude

had abandoned. And my cousin, Jean Pierre,
touched by God during the great wind,
found the rabbit he made of rags
and hid when he dreamed of the loup-garou,

who long ago ravaged the countryside.
That time is gone, the beast
reported dead, but in the nightmare
nothing ever changes. And nothing ever changes

in the fields we left for service in the city.
We watched a magpie on a stile,
the sun sheen on its wings,
the light like diamonds in the snow,

and we were happy, pressing our heads together,
hair blending at the attic window.
But one bird signifies danger. I wish
there had been three, to signify good journey.

For gifts are danger, the lady remarked,
when we went down for dinner. In the giver
they awaken only longing. That is why
I give what I would not want back.

The Witness

> inspired by Alberto Giacometti, *Selbstbildnis*, 1914

Every day as sunlight softened against the stones,
swallows came from the river
and I watched them from my window.
All that year I lay on my bed
or hobbled to and fro, dragged my body
from basin to book, book to beginning.
My hair grew long and curled about my ears.
I loved the chittering of the birds,
the slow glide of light across my window
as even more slowly my bones healed,
the bones that had snapped like saplings
when the stones rolled down on me
and the mountain opened. One day
I put on a coat, a tie, and began to draw myself—
the fine-etched mouth, the downcast eyes.
Now, as the seasons pass, all the forms
grow gaunt and flesh begins to vanish.
The cities are still at war. I behold
the twisted bodies stride forth into nightmare.

Beneath the Rain, the Pewter Feathers of the Seine

Where men in coarse blue jackets
or raveled sweaters take shelter
at corner overhangs, sell chestnuts
in paper cones, warming their hands
stirring the nuts slowly
lest they char on the braziers

where a woman gazes out the window
with her small scowling dog
in the café corner
sorting and peering at the coins
in her crocheted purse before
she orders another double crème

where the bookstalls are boarded
and in the cathedral with its rows and rows
of empty rush-bottom chairs
I can imagine
even Our Lady is lonely
as thin smoke rises from the offertory candles

where we walked once
in our wet overcoats
and you recited "Le Pont Mirabeau"
that was a narrow time for us
love
and sadness and your slow, deep voice

> *vienne la nuit sonne l'heure*
> *les jours s'en vont je demeure*
>
> > *night comes the hour sounds*
> > *the days pass I remain*

Liège, the Barges

Narcissi shiver, all in the same direction. A small gray dog cowers, its coat drenched, on the cobblestones down by the Meuse. The barges grow blacker; dark comes early or never leaves, and the clothes, washed and hung out days ago, are sodden, the blue sleeves of work shirts and the lank brown skirts of housewives hang like the hair of drowned men. Children with runny noses press their faces to smoky windows. Pancakes sizzle and sputter on the grease-caked, coal-black stoves beside the limp lace curtains, above aspidistras and leggy red geraniums that say *home*, that say *chez moi, me voici la femme*. And in the rain the sad river pocks and pebbles, river of a million million moments. In the rain the river slides endlessly. Nothing is as dirty as a slag heap in the rain. Still, beneath quilts they are warm on barges.

Everything I Sculpted

      after *Giacometti,* by Henri Cartier-Bresson

When I returned to my rooms,
forms began to flow through my hands.
The Lord spoke unto me—*Do not be afraid.*

Let your fingers coax the plaster
and clay into their proper
flowering. Everything I sculpted

became the flesh of the Lord. My own body,
bowed, with great splayed feet,
one hand cupping an elbow, the other

cupping my cheek. A pear, a boat,
a candle. Three figures
crossing a skeletal stage, eyes turned

up and inward. A gaunt grove
of trees, covered with lichen
and furred mosses, with which birds

make their nests,
and the birds themselves,
that sing the birth and death of worlds.

Then I walked out through the city,
coat pulled over my head in the rain,
to mark the start of my exile.

5

Mississippi Invocation

Come, green, fill our veins
    with tendrils and broad-lobed leaves,
        wave as the rain approaches, teach us
    the secret of swoon, exhaustion. Come,
great-petaled magnolias, scrotal figs
    in the crooks of branches, scarlet bells
        of Carolina creeper, bruised gardenias,
    mosses and lichens that fur the bark of oaks.
Come, fungi, come, buzzards,
    this teeming   is death   is teeming,
        the walls of our houses, the doors
    of our senses, dampen and soften.
Plunge us into sleep and deliquescence,
    we are sap and vine and solstice,
        ooze us, rot us, make us hot and hotter.
    Jasmine, wisteria, twine us, ensnare us,
stupefy us with your sugary blossoms.

Chant d'amour, 1965

I'm riding that bus again,
that same black bus again,
the man who wants to kill me
runs his hand along my thigh.
*Won't you get off the bus
and drink with me a little?*
Then he whispers to his buddies
and his hand grows more insistent.
Won't you get off for just a little while?

Next day I find his wallet
in my shoulder bag—

~~~

He put his wallet in my bag,
which hung open from my shoulder.
And there the story stops.
How could it go further?
But if I'd gone with him—?
My mother saw the photo in the paper,
the girl vanished from a Greyhound
headed toward Ventura,
her bones found in the desert.

Junked at dawn in the creosote—
no moon in the sky.

~~~

And if he'd been alone?
But his two slack-bellied friends
grinned at me with bad teeth.
He ran one hand along my thigh,

until I nearly climbed the window.
Still, I was tempted, just for the unknown.
For in those days, the world
could open out at any moment,
and none of it could hurt me.

Love Minus Zero

Harrumph harrumph, said my
Chaucer professor, pipe in his mouth,
pacing before the class on that

wintry afternoon, but I can't remember
what he was talking about—
probably *Troilus and Criseyde*—

harrumph harrumph, clearing his throat,
sex is enervating. I thought it was
way so cool, because in that room

full of virgins or putative virgins
I agreed with what I *believed*
he'd said: sex gave me *lots* of energy,

and I was delighted someone else
felt this way too. Making love
was the *best.* So when my new

boyfriend Jeff took me that April
in his scarlet Triumph TR3
to hear Dylan in Santa Monica,

and Dylan sang *Love Minus Zero/
No Limit*, in that huge dark auditorium
my heart soared, I might not

always be faithful but I was true
like ice, like fire. Like the song said.
And Jeff would know how true,

and the nubbin-sized baby
discovered in me the month before
when I went to the infirmary

with "flu" would someday know how true.
Ah, my little one whose father
Jeff was not, he was a generous boy,

nonetheless, who cuddled with me
on a madras bedspread beneath
a ceiling tapestry of Blake's "Tyger,"

helped me with a biology project,
and bought bags and bags of Fritos
when I had the munchies for salt.

Today, as the warblers trill outside
and the mourning doves coo, I believe
in love minus zero no limit as much as ever,

though Jeff vanished by summer,
my baby died in November, and that
enervated professor is long gone too.

These Things

In the final scene of Béjart's ballet
Siddhartha, a vast stage filled with
seething bodies slowly grows still

and sits in *Sukhasana*, breathing—
the way a child stops crying, sniffles,
subsides into sleep.

Time magazine reviewed the ballet
as corny and to say I wept
is corny but I did: wept and wept,

at twenty-two, in Belgium,
where my brand-new husband taught
to stay out of Vietnam. My child,

four years dead.
Of her birth in San Francisco I remember only
how they sent the pregnant nurse

from the room when they couldn't
find a heartbeat, how they
strapped me down because I fought

the ether cone and then
after, as they were wheeling me
to my room my mother

came toward me and I said *shit*
and felt guilty for swearing—
but earlier—when?

there were Dr. Quisici, hair on his arms,
blue and green paint, the baby scales,
and I thought, These things

I am seeing are here right now,
part of this time, this hospital room
where I will lose her.   Oh, but that's only

part of the reason I wept.
The bride and groom on the wedding cake—
lovely husband and wife, they thought.

So much pain, those years.
It is a relief to grow old—now that the blood
no longer comes, I can begin to think

beyond the sexual body. Buddhism,
says Cartier-Bresson,
consists in controlling the spirit

in order to attain harmony
and, through compassion,
to offer it to others. Sometimes

through the bedroom window
light falls on the antique patchwork kilim,
stains its patches honey-yellow—

or at dusk
beneath the pecan trees, fireflies.
And sometimes my monkey-mind thoughts

drop like leaves from a tree
and drift downstream as I sit in peace,
even if rain dashes the mountain

and a sly wind hisses at the windowsill.
It is not apart from darkness,
it is not different from emptiness.

Golden Shovel with One Tomato

Our tomatoes aren't growing this summer, so
we give them potting soil, mulch, more mulch, too much
fertilizer. You say they're knee-high? It depends

on whose knee—a two-year-old's maybe, but upon
my word I don't know what's wrong with a
raised bed garden that will only grow red

salvias, redbugs, red petunias. Maybe if I trade a wheelbarrow
of horse manure for one of my super-duper glazed
lemon bundt cakes with citron and candied orange peel, with

Andrew... or maybe if the damn rain
would just level off instead of flood and storm, and water
the garden the way it's supposed to... We're beside

ourselves. Just one tomato? Please? —Then the
summer tightens its grip, swamp-wet, white-
hot, and at last we retreat inside. Such chickens.

I Dreamed a Simple Story

So how am I supposed to give a lecture on Flannery O'Connor in an hour and a half when I

have been ordered to report at the police station because some old geezer saw my sweetheart and me lying in the sun half-clothed down a steep trail off the highway in a nearly hidden glade, and called the cops, who impounded our clothes so that I am wearing a bra and shirt and nothing more

don't know what high school this lecture is supposed to happen in because I am in a strange city, don't even know if the high school is in the city or somewhere out of town

and don't have the book, have not read it in years, have no lecture prepared, don't have my laptop to see if the person hosting the lecture has emailed me to tell me what high school I am supposed to be at

know only that Eric Cantor will be in the audience but which Eric Cantor this is, I do not know

wish I could take a rain check because here I am, in some strange person's house, pulling my shirt down around my ass and hoping my pubic hair doesn't show, and my sweetheart is saying *there's nothing to worry about* and I am snapping *oh yes there is* as this strange person's girlfriend gives me the stink eye

and somehow we are supposed to shower, show up at the station and get our clothes, figure out where the lecture is, figure out what to say, all this in an hour and a half

but it sure was beautiful, lying with my honey in that little clearing, and the glistening, impenetrable, nearly infinite forest below.

Sumac

Brilliant stems of sumac in a jam jar, black-eyed Susans—scarlet
tangled with gold—and blue ageratum, dusty Queen-Anne's-lace—

the flowers he brought when our son was born, and I loved them,
copious and wild, from the fields and hedgerows of the farm we
   lived on,

though by evening the acid sumac had killed everything, turned
   the water
rank and tannic. Driving to the airport today, passing sumac

like tongues of flame among the trees, I remember how pain
gave way to joy, back then, as I lay in my stitched cocoon of milk

and blood, the baby nestled on my chest listening as he had
listened all those summer months to the groundswell of my heart.

Wyrd

Like a summer creek the mother dries up
in me. Enough to see the sun and hear
the jays toward twilight squabbling in the pines.
Enough. All that worrying.

Clawfoot, bone, beak, and feather: now let be.

Sunlight, Sunlight

falling on him when I first knew him, as he leaned his head back, eyes shut, to the sun, in the Plymouth convertible. Falling on those strawberry fields that long-ago June twilight when we stopped after the violent thunderstorm, and on our muddy feet as we walked with our baskets, row after row. Falling on the berries, bruised, almost overripe, to be eaten quickly—then that night at the Monterey Inn, when I sat in the bathtub eating strawberries, strawberries, strawberries.

Sunlight doesn't stop just because we do. Hard to think there are lovers now who are just as new as we were. Sun is its own thing—may go out in a few billion years, as the scientist said, to which a lady in the front row gasped and asked him to repeat it. He did, and she replied, "Oh, thank God, I was afraid a moment ago you said a few *million*."

And here right now as I sit on this path on the campus where we teach, lawn equipment whirs around me, and students pass with their *Ah'm gone go* Southern soft voices and the *squich squich* of their flipflops—here right now, sun's all over this page except where shade is, sweet scalloped shade breaking the Mississippi glare. Rainbow on the page, the way my glasses and eyelashes reflect light, prismatically. And sunlight stroking the birds' throats so it comes out as song.

Return

But you *lived* here. You brought the baby home here,
      driving as if on eggs in the old yellow Plymouth
up the curving half-mile drive planted with daffodils,
      past the front lake with its Canada geese, past
the Angus bull in his field and the Angus cows in theirs,
      past the low white house and the swimming pool
nestled behind a squared-off boxwood hedge
      where, in summers, your kids were welcome to swim
from ten to noon (*chop chop, out by lunchtime!*
      your landlady, the famous beauty, would tell them)—
you brought the baby home to this tiny rented cottage
      on the vast estate south of Charlottesville, with its
three barns, its fields, the steep hill down to Ray's
      the farm manager's house, where his hound dog
flopped in the sun, and beyond Ray's into the forests.
      Your kids picked forget-me-notes down by the stream
that ran through the woods, and rambled around
      to find stuff for "The Nature Table"—lichen-furred
sticks, flaps of moss, a turtle shell, striate rocks,
      and once, lambs' tails, yes, actual curling lambs' tails
that had fallen off when Ray cut the circulation
      with rubber bands. Did you think it would not change?
Did you think the enormous king snake would still
      twine itself in August through the pool's boxwood,
and the cows would still bellow for their babies,
      and the children would still— Ah, there was sorrow
even then, fights sometimes, and because all but the baby
      were children of divorce, wracking sobs at partings,
did you think you could remember without pain?
      But there was so much love. And to go back
after nearly thirty years, and to see the fields empty,

    geese gone, cows gone, sheep gone, peeling paint
and broken windows on the big house, pool a stink
    of algae, flagstone terraces choked with weeds,
and your own little cottage derelict, capsized, moldy—
    you peered through a grimy window and what
did you see? A plastic doll, some trash, a box.
    Nothing, nothing. Not even the ghosts of children.

Ascending *les Gorges du Chassezac*

    Leaves' shadows against the rock at river bottom

        boulders

            tumbling water

    and paired butterflies

not quite yellow with not quite August

            on the trail, limeade-colored lizards

    a bottle-green dragonfly

        black moss, dry in the cracks of boulders

            smoky honey smell of beeboxes

halfway up at Albespeyres

        mistral blowing

    rain approaching

Mont Ventoux where Petrarch climbed

        we see it from the trailhead

            hazy blue on the horizon

    My husband stands beside me

Whatever is said is small, compared to silence

Acknowledgments

Many thanks to the editors of the following publications in which some of the poems in this collection appeared, sometimes in earlier versions or with different titles:

About Place: "Team Teaching at Parchman, Mississippi State Penitentiary"
Catamaran: "Rain"
Cave Wall: "Everything Here Looks Very Dismal"
Cerise: "We Came Home Over the Snowy Fields for Christmas"
Cutthroat: "These Things"
Diode: "October: A Gigan," "Love Minus Zero," "Minyas' Daughters," "*Yahrzeit*"
Earth Tones: "Sunlight, Sunlight"
Ekphrasis: "Patio with Black Door"
Jung Journal: Culture and Psyche: "Solstice"
Many Mountains Moving: "Ascending *les Gorges du Chassezac*" (as "*Les Gorges du Chassezac*")
Mom Egg Review: "I Dreamed a Simple Story" (as "A Simple Tale"), "In That Kitchen (She Speaks to Herself)"
Poetry Kanto: "Yugen"
Poetry South: "The Frescoes of San Dalmazzo"
Prairie Schooner: "Letter to Emma Bovary," "Wyrd"
Redheaded Stepchild: "Beneath the Rain, the Pewter Feathers of the Seine," "Shelterhouse"
Runes: "Cold Fire"
TAB: The Journal of Poetry and Poetics: "Chant d'amour, 1965," "Nearly April"
Two Thirds North: "Haecceitas" (as "After Christopher Smart")
Valparaiso Poetry Review: "Mayumi," "Sister," "Sumac"
VOX: "Liège, the Barges" (as "Liège, the Barges, Rain")
Vox Populi: "Prayer"

"Everything Here Looks Very Dismal" was published in *The Traveler's Vade Mecum*, ed. Helen Klein Ross (Red Hen Press, 2016).

"Mississippi Invocation" (as "Solstice: Mississippi Invocation") and "Return" were published in *The Practicing Poet: Writing Beyond the Basics*, ed. Diane Lockward (Terrapin Books, 2018).

"Sundown" (as "Sundown, Savannah") was published in *Stone River Sky: An Anthology of Georgia Poems*, eds. Cary Scott Wilkerson and Melissa Dickson (Negative Capability, 2015).

"Sunlight, Sunlight" was made into a broadside for a reading at Goshen College, Indiana.

"Sunlight, Sunlight" was reprinted in the chapbook *First, earth*, which was published in *The Chapbook*, Number 5, ed. Alan May (Knoxville, 2014).

"Vicksburg National Military Park" was commissioned by the American Academy of Poets for the Imagine Your Parks Grant, 2016.

My warm thanks to all those who have helped make this book a reality: the writing community at the University of Mississippi and Square Books in Oxford; the members of my online workshop, with whom I have traded poems for many years; and, always, my family. I spent wonderful residencies at the Djerassi Resident Artists Program and CAMAC/Centre d'Art, Marnay, during the shaping of this book. Some of these poems came into existence during poetry workshops at the Squaw Valley Community of Writers, and I am grateful to my fellow poets and Robert Hass for their critiques. And especially to Diane Lockward, for choosing *The Bones of Winter Birds*.

About the Author

Ann Fisher-Wirth is the author of five previous books of poetry. Her fifth book, *Mississippi*, is a poetry/ photography collaboration with Maude Schuyler Clay (Wings Press, 2018). With Laura-Gray Street, she co-edited *The Ecopoetry Anthology* (Trinity UP, 2013). Her work appears in such journals as *Prairie Schooner, Diode*, and *Valparaiso Poetry Review*. Her awards include two Mississippi Arts Commission fellowships and the Mississippi Institute of Arts and Letters Poetry Award. She was also awarded a 1994-1995 Fulbright to Fribourg, Switzerland, and was 2002-2003 Fulbright Distinguished Chair of American Studies at Uppsala, Sweden. She has had residencies at Djerassi, Hedgebrook, Mesa Refuge, and CAMAC in France, and was the 2017 Anne Spencer Poet-in-Residence at Randolph College. A senior Black Earth Institute fellow and member of the board, she teaches and directs the Environmental Studies minor at the University of Mississippi, and also teaches yoga in Oxford, Mississippi.

www.annfisherwirth.com

www.ingramcontent.com/pod-product-compliance
Lightning Source LLC
Chambersburg PA
CBHW020144130526
44591CB00030B/215